MEDITATIONS
ON THE
STABAT
MATER

Armand de Malleray, FSSP

*All booklets are published
thanks to the generosity of the supporters
of the Catholic Truth Society*

CATHOLIC
TRUTH
SOCIETY

PUBLISHERS
TO THE
HOLY
SEE

Imprimi Potest: Very Reverend Andrzej Komorowski,
FSSP, Superior General
Fribourg, Switzerland, 12th February 2021

Nihil Obstat: Reverend David Potter, *Censor Deputatus*
Liverpool, England, 7th April 2021

Imprimatur: Most Reverend Malcolm McMahon OP,
Archbishop of Liverpool,
Liverpool, England, 12th April 2021

All biblical quotations are taken from the Douay Rheims Edition.

IMAGE CREDITS:

Cover: *Christ on the Cross with Mary, John and Mary Magdalene* by the Master of the Life of the Virgin. Wallraf-Richartz-Museum & Fondation Corboud. Photo © Rheinisches Photo Archive Cologne, rba_c002405.

Page 4: *Christ Carrying the Cross, with the Crucifixion* by Gerard David. Robert Lehman Collection, 1975. The Metroplitan Museum of Art.

Page 7: *Christ Bearing the Cross*, North Netherlandish. Bequest of George D. Pratt, 1935. The Metroplitan Museum of Art.

Page 12: *The Crucifixion with the Virgin, Saint John, Saint Jerome, and Saint Mary Magdalene* [middle panel] by Pietro Perugino. Andrew W. Mellon Collection, The National Gallery of Art, Washington.

Page 38: *The Crucifixion* by Jan Provost.The Jack and Belle Linsky Collection, 1982. The Metroplitan Museum of Art.

Page 62: *The Lamentation of Christ* by Simon Marmion. Robert Lehman Collection, 1975. The Metroplitan Museum of Art.

Page 76: *The Resurrection* by Gerard David. Robert Lehman Collection, 1975. The Metroplitan Museum of Art.

ISBN 978 1 78469 740 2

Contents

Foreword

If you truly wish to be transformed by Christ, go to the Cross and contemplate his Passion. If you truly desire to plumb the depths of knowledge of Christ's Passion, go to his Blessed Mother. There is no other created being in heaven or on earth that understands the sufferings of Our Lord better than the one who had a sword pierce her own heart. If you want to know some of what the Blessed Virgin Mary teaches about her Son's Passion, read this book. With great wisdom, Rev Fr Armand de Malleray has chosen the hymn which best expresses the profound sorrow of Our Lady, a sorrow filled with hope – the *Stabat Mater*. This hymn forms the landscape in which he skilfully illustrates the mystery of Calvary and the journey of the soul from fall to rise.

MOTHER MARILLA OSB,
Superior General of the Tyburn Nuns

True devotion to Blessed Mary Ever-Virgin is the simplest, safest, and straightest way to loving union with Christ, and contemplation of the compassionate heart of "the Lady of fair weeping" leads us directly to the Heart of her divine Son, pierced by our sins; it has the power to move us to contrition, to the desire to make reparation, and to a greater assurance of Our Lord's merciful love. This conviction of faith inspired Jacopone da Todi's writing of his hymn, the *Stabat Mater*, and animates Fr de Malleray's new commentary, so clear and sound in its doctrine and lyrical in its language. This beautiful little book, born of prayer, is just what I need, what every Catholic needs, for the fruitful praying of the Stations of the Cross.

FR JOHN SAWARD,
Blackfriars Hall, Oxford, author of
Redeemer in the Womb: Jesus Living in Mary

Stabat Mater

Below is the English translation of the *Stabat Mater* used in this commentary. It is a more literal rendering than the traditional and well-known version by Fr Edward Caswell CO. Whilst some of the poetic feel Fr Caswell was able to convey in his beloved translation is lost, this version reveals more of what is happening in the original Latin text, and is therefore more fruitful for commentary. However, Fr Caswell's translation is still preferable as a text for devotion, and so is included at the end of this book for use in private prayer and meditation (see page 73).

The Sorrowful Mother was standing
in tears beside the Cross
as her Son was hanging

Her soul was full of grief
and anguish and sorrow,
for a sword pierced [it].

How sad and how afflicted
was that blessed One,
the Mother of an only Son!

How she grieved and lamented,
the faithful Mother as she saw
the pangs of her glorious Son.

Who is there who would not weep,
were he to see Christ's Mother
in such great torment?

Who could not feel compassion
when thinking of Christ's Mother
sorrowing with her Son?

For the sins of her own people
she saw Jesus in agony
and broken by the scourging.

She saw the dear One born of her
all the time He was dying and abandoned
until He gave up the ghost.

Come then Mother, you fount of love,
my grasping the intensity of [your] sorrow
grant, that I may mourn with you.

Make my heart burn
with love for Christ, [my] God,
that I may find grace before Him.

O holy Mother, this achieve:
impress the wounds of the Crucified One
deep in my very heart.

Of your wounded Begotten One,
for He deigned to suffer so much for me,
Let me share with you the pangs.

Grant me to weep lovingly with you;
to feel the pains of the Crucified One
as long as I live.

To stand with you beside the Cross
and to be with you united
in grief: that, I desire.

Virgin without equal among virgins,
be not to me bitter;
grant that I may mourn with you.

Grant that I carry about the dying state
    of Christ;
grant that I be a sharer in [His] Passion;
grant that I relive [His] wounds.

Grant that I be wounded with [His] wounds;
let the Cross inebriate me,
and also the blood of the Son.

That I might not burn and be consumed
    in the flames,
be a defence to me, O Virgin,
on judgement day.

O Christ, when I must depart hence,
give me through the Mother to seize
the palm of victory.

When my body is dead,
grant that my soul be given
the glory of paradise. Amen.

'The Sorrowful Mother was standing'

"Stabat mater dolorosa – The Sorrowful Mother was standing." This first line of one of the most celebrated Catholic hymns conjures up the sad melody sung by millions of Catholics for over eight centuries when walking from one station of the Cross to the next. Attributed to the Franciscan friar Jacopone da Todi (1230-1306), the *Stabat Mater* has sustained the devotion of countless believers. Learned and simple folks alike have contemplated the pious depiction of the crucified Saviour and of his Sorrowful Mother, culminating in their joint offering at Calvary. The *Stabat Mater* teaches us that every fallen child of Adam and Eve benefits from uniting sacrificially with Jesus and Mary.

Holy Church granted her stamp of approval when including the *Stabat Mater* in her official liturgy as the Sequence at the *Mass of the Seven Sorrows of Mary*[1] (15th September). Its lyrics have inspired the greatest composers, such as Palestrina, Charpentier, Vivaldi,

---

[1] The references are to the Extraordinary Form of the Roman Rite, both the missal and the breviary.

Pergolesi, Haydn, Rossini, Dvořák, Verdi, Poulenc and Arvo Pärt. The *Stabat Mater* elaborates on the prophecy of the old man Simeon in the Temple of Jerusalem, stating that a "*sword of anguish*" was to pierce the heart of the Blessed Virgin Mary (*Luke* 2:35). A mirror image to this hymn is the less known *Stabat Mater Speciosa*, (*The Beauteous Mother was Standing*), echoing the joys of the Blessed Virgin Mary at the Nativity of the Lord. *Jam toto Subitus* (*Now Let the Darkling Eve*) is a later summary of the *Stabat Mater* in a mere six strophes ascribed to Callisto Palumbella. Endowed with a poignant plainchant melody from the eighteenth century, it is still part of Vespers on the feast of the Seven Sorrows of the Blessed Virgin Mary.

The best known original version of the *Stabat Mater* comprises twenty stanzas of three verses each, hence sixty verses, grouped in three parts of eight, ten and two stanzas respectively. Each first two verses numbers eight syllables, against seven syllables only for every last verse of each stanza. It makes the stanzas sound less repetitive, conveying a sense of incompletion and of bounce. The two first verses of each stanza rhyme, as well as the last verse of every two consecutive stanzas: -A, -A, C; -B, -B, -C. This subtle concatenation groups stanzas two by two in sub-entities of six verses. Part One (stanzas one to eight) describes the Crucifixion as seen by an anonymous narrator. In Part Two (stanzas

nine to eighteen), a contrite sinner implores the Blessed
Virgin Mary. Part Three (stanzas nineteen and twenty)
concludes with a penitent's petition to Christ.[2]

The structure of the hymn is telling: Part One
describes the situation; Part Two connects us with the
Blessed Mother; and Part Three emboldens us to address
her Son personally. Thus, the very composition sets Our
Lady as Mediatrix (Part Two) between us (Part One)
and Christ (Part Three). We can only enter Paradise
through Christ; but we cannot be heard by Christ unless
his Mother enlivens our soul with the sorrow we need
to experience for the sake of our own sins. In the *Stabat
Mater*, the Blessed Virgin Mary teaches us sorrow as
the condition for salvation. It must not be selfish or
sentimental sorrow. Instead, it must be sorrow born
from the realisation of our guilt and grown through trust
in God's forgiveness and mercy.

The *Stabat Mater* incites the gradual acknowledging
of guilt by establishing a filial relationship between the
penitent onlooker and the Mournful Mother, leading to
a brotherly relationship with Christ Crucified recognised
as the Brother we slew and as the Messiah who saves.
These realisations, as they restructure the individual's
relationships with God, the world and himself, lead to

---

[2] An alternative version used by Giovanni Pierluigi da Palestrina
(c. 1525-1594) does not include the final address to Christ, but
focuses on Our Lady all along.

the awakening of the moral conscience. Let us examine in more detail each of the three parts.

Part One: The *Stabat Mater* teaches us to say 'I'. What 'I' will speak, though? Not our inflated ego, inherited from the sinful pride of Adam and Eve. Not the rebellious 'I', setting itself against the divine Father and trampling underfoot God's law of life in a hellish brag: "*I shall not serve!*" Instead, the humble and filial 'I' will be heard: that 'I' healed through guilt confessed and through filiation restored, as illustrated by the parable of the Prodigal Son: "*Father, I have sinned against heaven and before thee*" (*Luke* 15:18). In that perspective, the anonymity of the narrator in Part One is loaded with deep meaning. No one says 'I' in Part One. No one dares or is able to take ownership for the words spoken. The vacant identity of the narrator indicates that sin has nearly killed the moral conscience. It is too weak to act. This stage could be called purgative. The selfish ego is incapacitated by the display of the Mother's sorrow. That sinful ego is silenced by the detailed description of what the innocent Lady endures. And yet, already it benefits from absorbing the bitter depiction of the Sorrowful Mother. These stanzas correct the selfish use of emotions. They turn sentimentality into sensitivity and mere consciousness into conscience.

Part Two: Following this purgation, an essential improvement occurs in the healing process. One could name this stage illuminative. A relationship is established. It connects the onlooker and the Mother as he starts contemplating her. No longer anonymous, he discovers his identity as her spiritual child. He accepts responsibility for her sufferings, endured by her for his sake in union with her Crucified Son. The gradual admitting of his personal guilt is painful. To the soul's surprise, however, this realisation does not crush it but liberates it. Where he feared confrontation with a harsh or exacting judge, the penitent only contemplates a beautiful Woman in tears. Instead of suffering humiliation, he is granted enlightenment. If this revelation hurts when it occurs, it also heals. This new filiation instils in the soul a peace that is subtle but all-powerful, a joy discreet but unmistakable. Such rewards consign to oblivion the coarse pleasures of sin, held up to then as the measure of human fulfilment. The unidentified self of Part One grows into the self-confessed penitent child of the Mother in Part Two. This leads him to address her divine Son in Part Three.

Part Three: The Sorrowful Mother acted as a protective lens between the dying ego of the sinner and Christ, the Splendour of the Father. Now is the unitive stage, between the soul and Christ. Like the Blue Madonna on the Great Window of Chartres Cathedral, the Mater Dolorosa is a merciful prism, granting time for the eyes of the muddy pilgrim to open wider and to welcome the blazing beams of the Sun of Justice, Jesus the Saviour. Thus is the personal and direct encounter between the penitent soul and Christ made possible in the last two stanzas of the *Stabat Mater*.

We should not take for granted our relationship with Christ. While He (and his Mother) always will this bond for our good, we sinners need all their care to understand and accept it. If the penitent is emboldened to address Christ directly in Part Three, such improvement is necessarily owed to the Mother's intercession in Parts One and Two. Without it, the soul would proudly deny its guilt or collapse in dire shame at the mere thought of direct contact with her Son, now undeniably identified as the God pierced by our sins. Yet out of necessity for salvation, the guilty soul must relate to Christ, the only Saviour of men. Becoming the child of Mary is the only way. Marian filiation is what allows personal encounter with Christ. Since the Crucified Saviour is also, and supremely, Son of the Virgin, kinship gives the penitent assurance of mercy. Brotherhood bodes well for pardon. Let us now examine step by step this liberating process.

Part One – His Mother

This is a very general description which could just as well apply to any mother, including those of Gestas and Dismas, the two thieves crucified next to Our Lord. Perhaps their mothers also stood by the crosses of their own sons. No doubt they would have suffered grievously to see their sons die in so much pain.

Verse 1
Stabat mater dolorosa
The Sorrowful Mother was standing

The very first word of the hymn is '*Stabat*' – in English: 'She was standing'. Upright station as a physical posture expresses the moral strength of the Blessed Virgin Mary, standing firm in her faith and hope. It warns us from the onset against a possible misinterpretation of the pathos which follows: the forthcoming weeping and grieving betray no superficial or weak sentimentality, but saintly compassion after that of God's own heart ever compassionate for sinners. Since 'she stood', as eyewitness St John testifies (*John* 19:25), artistic depictions of Our Lady swooning at the foot of the Cross are not consistent with Scripture.

Verse 2
juxta Crucem lacrimosa
in tears beside the Cross

Our Lady stands 'by' ('*juxta*') the Cross of her Son. Spatial proximity expresses redemptive closeness since the New Eve is associated with the New Adam as our co-redemptrix, in radical subordination to him. By contrast, in the Garden of Eden closeness turned into complicity. The first Eve stood near the forbidden tree whose fruit she shared with the first Adam, for their demise and that of all their posterity.

The New Eve is 'tearful' ('*lacrimosa*') as her Son is bleeding. Mary sheds tears while her Son sheds his blood. Both fluids thus express the compassion of their hearts and are life-giving, like heavenly dew and seed.

Verse 3
dum pendebat Filius
as her Son was hanging

The word 'Son' ('*Filius*') appears at the very end of this first stanza, while the word 'Mother' occurred as its second word. This textual estrangement between the Mother and the Son echoes the pressure of evil trying to separate the loving unity of the two hearts – but in vain as explained in verse 2.

The stanza ends depicting the posture of the Son, hanging, thus offering a suggestive parallel with its opening when the Mother was introduced as standing. Both characters are in a vertical position, but the Mother stands on her feet while the Son hangs on the nails. Standing is to Mary hardly less painful than is hanging for Jesus, though; while hanging betrays no less strength in Jesus than standing does for Mary, since the Lord chose and willed this passive posture to redeem the world through his obedience: "'*And I, if I be lifted up from the earth, will draw all things to myself.' (Now this he said, signifying what death he should die)*" (*John* 12:32-33).

SECOND STANZA

Verse 4

Cuius animam gementem
Her soul was full of grief

Whereas the first stanza described the scene externally, this second one now introduces us into the very soul of the Sorrowful Mother. Why this important progress into her intimacy? Vain curiosity or impious indiscretion can have no part in it. The only legitimate and fruitful purpose is to better appreciate her grief so as to be shaped by it, her sorrowful heart becoming the mould for our souls as they learn contrition.

Verse 5
contristatam et dolentem
and anguish and sorrow

From a natural perspective, Our Lady suffers by virtue of the bond of motherhood uniting her with her tortured Son. Every mother wants the good of her child. Her Son Jesus is in pain. Hence, his Mother suffers. Since the Immaculate is the only mother uncontaminated by sin, her natural love is considerably purer than the love of any other mother. The natural love of a mother for her child can indeed be tragically stunted, as shown in the millions of unforced abortions when the mother says of her child: "To me this is nobody: you can dispose of it." Whereas unborn children bear no personal guilt, we sinners do. And yet, Our Lady will not disavow us, on the contrary, she will suffer for us. Her natural grief for Jesus is the vehicle for her supernatural suffering with Him and for us. She knows that He undergoes his Passion freely in order to save us from sin. She wills to support his design fully, thus contributing to our salvation.

Verse 6
pertransivit gladius
for a sword pierced [it]

This sword is the sword of anguish once prophesied by the old man Simeon at the Presentation of the Child Jesus in the Temple of Jerusalem, when he warned the young Mother: "*And thy own soul a sword shall pierce, that, out of many hearts thoughts may be revealed*" (*Luke* 2:35). The mention of the word 'sword' in this hymn points to Our Lady, albeit indirectly. Although any mother would experience moral pain when witnessing her son's execution, the reference to the Gospel of St Luke's prophecy in the Temple narrows the identification to the Mother and Son *par excellence*. At the Nativity of Jesus, the Blessed Virgin as the New Eve was spared the birth pangs undergone by Eve of old and by all her daughters as a consequence of sin. But at Calvary, Our Lady gives birth in dire pains to the multitude of those to be saved by the death of her Son. The sword of sorrow piercing her soul (with her full and generous consent) establishes within her a motherly bond offered to each and every human for their spiritual gestation until eventual birth into blessed eternity. Here we see a similarity between the sacraments of our spiritual birth represented by the pierced side of Our Lord, and the Mother of all Christians whose heart was also pierced.

This third stanza parallels the miracle of the son of the widow of Nain (*Luke 7:11-17*):

When he came nigh to the gate of the city, behold a dead man was carried out, the only son of his mother; and she was a widow: and a great multitude of the city was with her. Whom when the Lord had seen, being moved with mercy towards her, he said to her: "Weep not." And he came near and touched the bier. And they that carried it, stood still. And he said: "Young man, I say to thee, arise." And he that was dead, sat up, and began to speak. And he gave him to his mother.

At Nain, no doubt Our Lord was moved with compassion not only for the anonymous mother before his eyes, but also and principally for his own holy Mother whose grief at his own death He foresaw. How moving to see Him console in advance his Sorrowful Mother, also a widow, assuring that her only-begotten Son will be given back to her – or her to Him – once risen from the dead.

Verse 7

O quam tristis et afflicta
How sad and how afflicted

This verse describes the pitiable state of mind of the Mother, in sharp contrast with her condition as 'Blessed'.

But her sadness is never self-centred. On the contrary, it is intercessory and co-redemptive. She weeps on our behalf.

Verse 8
fuit illa benedicta
was that blessed one

This conjures up the happy memories – of the Annunciation; of Our Lady's Visitation to her cousin Elizabeth with the hymn of joy, Mary's *Magnificat*; the glorious Nativity proclaimed by the angels and worshipped by the kings of the Orient; Mary's successful intervention on behalf of the newlyweds at Cana, obtaining from her Son his first miracle on their behalf – and suggests so many other big and small joys not recorded in the Holy Gospels.

Verse 9
mater Unigeniti
the mother of an only Son

Being the Mother of Jesus is the reason why Elizabeth calls Our Lady blessed: "*Blessed art thou among women and blessed is the fruit of thy womb. And whence is this to me that the mother of my Lord should come to me?*" (*Luke* 1:42-43). But Jesus is also called Mary's 'firstborn' because, while she was a biological Mother to Him only, on Calvary she became spiritually the Mother of all the redeemed. This adoption of us by the Mother was commanded by Our Lord when entrusting St John to Mary: "*Woman, behold thy son*" (*John* 19:26). Whereas in Bethlehem Our Lady as the New Eve had been spared the penalty of suffering when giving birth to Our Lord, the New Adam, on Calvary she begot us mystically through her sufferings.

Our Lord once referred to the pangs of childbirth leading to motherly joy as an analogy with spiritual desolation leading to eternal joys:

> *A woman, when she is in labour, hath sorrow, because her hour is come; but when she hath brought forth the child, she remembereth no more the anguish, for joy that a man is born into the world. So also you now indeed have sorrow: but I will see you again and your heart shall rejoice. And your joy no man shall take from you* (*John* 16:21-22).

In his prescience, Our Lord would have known that this would apply to his Sorrowful Mother spiritually begetting us at the foot of the Cross. St John the Apostle, given by Jesus to his Mother at Calvary as the firstborn of their joint sufferings, seems to echo this truth in his *Apocalypse* when he describes the mysterious Woman, a figure of the Church collectively and of Our Lady individually: "*And being with child, she cried travailing in birth: and was in pain to be delivered*" (*Rv* 12:2). It is essential to realise that Our Lady's moral sufferings made possible her spiritual motherhood towards all the redeemed. Her tears were as essential to beget us to grace, just as her virginal womb was to conceive Our Lord. St Monica had tirelessly prayed for the conversion of her wayward son Augustine. In filial gratitude towards his pious mother, the great doctor of the Church acknowledged himself as *the son of [her] tears*.[3] How much more literally every Christian soul could apply this to Our Lady's tears at Calvary!

The title of a modern autobiography, *A Tear Saved Me*, by Angèle Lieby (2014), offers a variation on this theme. The author explains how she was imprisoned in her own body during her artificial coma, unable to show any sign of consciousness while she heard and understood everything around her. Having given up on her, the doctors were about to 'unplug' her. Her pregnant daughter spoke in her ear, begging her to recover so as to see her grandchild later to be born. The daughter then saw a tear roll down from her mother's eye. Her tear proved that Angèle was conscious and saved her. Similarly, the thought of us, her children, caused Our Lady's tears[4] as she kept interceding for us[5] after the

---

3   *Confessions*, Book III, Chapter 12.

4   Our Lady principally wept for her Son Jesus suffering on the Cross. But knowing that He suffered for us sinners, she embraced his intention and consequently wept over us.

5   Not for herself, who had been saved preveniently by her Son.

Accuser had pronounced us morally dead and beyond recovery from sin.

FOURTH STANZA

Unlike the women of Jerusalem on the way to Calvary, the Blessed Mother weeps not over her Son, as if she does not understand or support His Sacrifice, but rather, through her compassion for Him, she weeps over us her spiritual progeny, because our sins destroy us: "*And there followed Him a great multitude of people and of women, who bewailed and lamented Him. But Jesus turning to them, said: 'Daughters of Jerusalem, weep not over me; but weep for yourselves and for your children'*" (Luke 23:27-28).

Verse 10
Quæ moerebat et dolebat
How she grieved and lamented

Like Our Lord, Our Lady experienced emotions according to a human nature unhampered by sin. There is not a hint of selfishness in her grief – no more than in her past joys. She is all compassion, as at her *Magnificat* she was all thanksgiving without pride. Wailing was an expected part of mourning for middle-eastern women: however, it is much more likely that Our Lady would have grieved silently, as best befitted her dignity and the depth of her sorrow.

Verse 11
pia Mater, dum videbat
the faithful mother as she saw

Beyond his physical sufferings, the Mother understood the moral torments of Jesus as He took upon Himself the burden of guilt for each and every sin ever committed or to be committed by men until the end of history. Our Lady is referred to eight times as 'Mother' in the *Stabat Mater*, and twice as 'Virgin'; but never as 'Woman', which is, however, the way Our Lord addressed her from the Cross, and at Cana. This is due to the fact that the *Stabat Mater* does not depict her from the perspective of Our Lord but as contemplated by us sinners. Only the New Adam can address the New Eve as the feminine type of mankind redeemed: 'Woman'. We sinners can only refer to her as to the Virgin and Mother.

Verse 12
nati poenas inclyti
the pangs of her glorious Son

The Latin adjective '*inclytus*' translates as 'great, illustrious'. Only faith allows the Blessed Virgin to discern the glory of her Son as Saviour, contrary to his most abject appearance. In this verse, the word '*poenas*' ('pangs') is poetically inserted between '*nati*' (Son) and '*inclyti*' ('glorious'), like each nail hammered into the limbs of Our Lord; but also like Our Lord's Body as embraced by the compassion of his Mother. '*Nati*' and *inclyti*' then figure the two arms of the Mother affirming that this tortured Victim ('*poenas*') is fundamentally her Son ('*nati*'), and a glorious Son ('*inclyti*'). The insertion of 'poenas' in the middle of the verse is a protestation of love, a manifesto of faith.

FIFTH STANZA

Verse 13

Quis est homo qui non fleret
Who is there who would not weep

For the first time, the identity of the viewer is enquired about. After the neutral description of the beginning (first stanza) the poem later focused on the feelings of Our Lady (second to fourth stanza), but only in this fifth stanza is a third party mentioned. Note that this is done in the most impersonal way, through a general interrogation to the reader.

Verse 14

Matrem Christi si videret
were he to see Christ's Mother

Significantly, the hypothetical witness is not expected to weep over Christ – named here for the very first time – but over his Mother. This does not mean that the sufferings of Mary are more important than those of Jesus. He is the Redeemer, while she is only co-redemptrix in radical subordination to Him. If the Virgin Mary's sufferings must move us prior to those of her Son, it is because ordinary sinners are more likely to sympathise with the grief of an innocent woman and of a mother. A mother's sorrow strikes a chord even in sinful hearts, awakening a filial bond of gratitude and proximity experienced by a child long before he would commit his first sin.

Verse 15
in tanto supplicio
in such great torment

Since the sinner knows that the Mother is innocent, he is more likely to admit the injustice of her sufferings. While the heinous crowd accuses the Son of being an imposter and a blasphemer, no one suggests that his Mother is at fault. Even average sinners admit this and thus, they will object to her moral tortures. This is a non-committal but necessary first step towards confessing that we, sinners, are the cause of the Mother's grief. However, the *Stabat Mater* will reveal this truth after several more stanzas, because the reader is still morally too weak to bear such a realisation.

SIXTH STANZA

This stanza deepens the meaning of the previous one. Each of the three verses must be read in contrast with the three previous verses. It invites us to interiorise the emotion.

Verse 16

Quis non posset contristari
Who could not feel compassion

Verse 13 also began with this question ('*Quis*': 'Who'), but it only described the *external* expression of sorrow, namely, the tears. Verse 16 now asks about the *internal* cause for tears, namely, sympathy as experienced within the soul.

Verse 17

Christi Matrem contemplari
when thinking of Christ's Mother

While verse 14 referred to the Mother of Christ as merely 'seen' ('*videret*'), verse 17 invites us to meditate on her attentively ('*contemplari*'). Again, this deepens the perspective from external to internal; from what appears to the eyes of the body to what the eyes of the soul should discover.

Verse 18
dolentem cum Filio
sorrowing with her Son

Verse 15 described the torment ('*supplicio*') undergone by Our Lady. Verse 18 focuses on its spiritual nature, namely, her compassion for her Son.

SEVENTH STANZA

Only in this penultimate stanza of Part One is the cause for such suffering introduced: the sin of the people. It is striking that up to then no mention is made of the fact that the Son is innocent, and that He dies to redeem the sinful human race. Pedagogically, the poem avoids charging the reader with guilt from the start and only displays before his eyes the spectacle of undeserved suffering.

Verse 19
Pro peccatis suæ gentis
For the sins of her own people

The possessive adjective 'her' ('*suæ*') entails a rich signification. It reminds us that the Blessed Virgin belongs to the sinful race of Adam, from whose stain she was exempted through her Immaculate Conception, a privilege befitting her divine motherhood. On the other hand, her kinship enables her to expiate on behalf of her fallen fellow-humans and to intercede for them, as did Esther and Judith in the Old Testament prefiguring Our Lady.

vidit Iesum in tormentis
she saw Jesus in agony

The only mention of the Holy Name occurs in this verse 20, that is, exactly one third into the sixty-verse long hymn. Our Lady learnt from Archangel Gabriel at her Annunciation that she was to name her child by that name: "*Behold thou shalt conceive in thy womb and shalt bring forth a son: and thou shalt call his name Jesus*" (*Luke* 1:31). 'Jesus' means 'Saviour'. It is fitting that the Holy Name should appear right after the first mention of sin in the previous verse, for sin is the illness and 'Jesus-Saviour' is the remedy. From the start the Sorrowful Mother would have known that the salvation her Son brought was from sin, not from the Roman occupiers – that is, from spiritual oppression, not political – and would be wrought at a painful cost.

Verse 21
et flagellis subditum
and broken by the scourging

The scourging obviously refers to an earlier stage in the Passion, in the courtyard of Pontius Pilate, before the way of the Cross. This is the only mention in the *Stabat Mater* of the torments inflicted upon Our Lord prior to his Crucifixion. It reminds us that Our Lady accompanied her divine Son all along his Passion, not only at Calvary. As verse 6 stated, quoting Simeon's prophecy about a sword of suffering, as early as in Our Lord's infancy Our Lady knew that her role as his Mother entailed a sharing in his sacrifice. She would have known it from the Annunciation and probably before, as announced by the prophets (e.g. Isaiah's 'Suffering Servant', Chapter 53; or King David's Psalm 21).

EIGHTH STANZA

This stanza concludes Part One. As an intended signal, for the first time the three verses end with the same rhyme ('-tum').

Verse 22

Vidit suum dulcem Natum
She saw the dear One born of her

This verse could aptly describe the Nativity. '*Natum*' explicitly refers to childbirth. In this context, it fittingly reminds us that the Crib only prepared the Cross. The author of the *Stabat Mater*, Jacopone da Todi, was a Franciscan, a religious order credited with having invented the Nativity devotion of Christmas cribs.

Verse 23
moriendo desolatum
all the time He was dying and abandoned

Our Lady stayed on, supporting her divine Child all his life and above all as He hung on the Cross for three hours, as expressed by '*moriendo*' ('He was dying'), which implies a process rather than an instantaneous event.

Verse 24
dum emisit spiritum
until He gave up the ghost

Our Lady witnessed the first breath taken by her Child on his Birth in Bethlehem. She witnesses his last breath as well on the Cross. When the Passion is sung liturgically, a pause occurs at that moment and all kneel down, for this is the very instant of the redemption of the entire world. This is when the two main components in the human nature of the Lord Jesus, namely his Body and his Soul, undergo the fateful separation called death. But the divinity of Jesus remains united to either component, albeit separately, until their reunion at the Resurrection on Easter morning.

This verse concludes Part One of the *Stabat Mater*, characterised by its descriptive outlook offered through the eyes of a non identified narrator. From a moral perspective, Part One was non-committal. It plainly presented the facts as externally considered. Noticing this is important if one is to appreciate the significance of the shift from narration to speech occurring in Part Two, expressing a dramatic escalation.

Part Two – My Mother

NINTH STANZA

For the very first time, a personal address to the Mother occurs, taking the form of a plea. This decisive shift from factual narrative to direct speech expresses a moral awakening whereby the attentive spectator of Part One gradually turns into a repentant actor in the drama.

Verse 25

Eia, Mater, fons amoris
Come then mother, you fount of love

'*Eia*' is an interjection expressing encouragement. As a direct address to the Holy Mother (with the vocative '*Mater*'), it calls for an identified subject uttering this invocation. Such identification is a blessing received from the Mother, here invoked as 'fount of love'. In Part One, to remain external to her sufferings and to those of her Son denoted a lack of love. Conversely, to establish a personal relationship with her and her Son now indicates the first stage of true love. That love is flowing from her to the narrator who gradually recognises her as the 'fount' of all love, inasmuch as she conceived, carried and offered for all men Love incarnate, her Son Jesus.

Verse 26

me sentire vim doloris
my grasping the intensity of [your] sorrow

At last, the impersonal narrator of Part One is revealed as a truly personal 'me'. So far there were only 'She' and 'He'. Now we discover an 'I' and a 'You'. This development is very meaningful as it illustrates the awakening of the moral conscience of the reader. He realises that this moving story is also *his* story. From a mere narrator, he is transformed into a participant. In our English translation of this verse we deliberately avoid the personal pronoun 'I' because the Latin original saves its dramatic occurrence for the next verse.

Verse 27

fac, ut tecum lugeam
grant, that I may mourn with you

The imperative mode (*'fac'*, 'grant') is yet a further step in the identification of a personal onlooker. This is improved with the 'tecum' – 'with you' and finally achieved with the *'lugeam'* – 'I may mourn'. Now, and only now, about in the middle of the entire poem, is the

'I' revealed. It is the first explicit admission of the reader's personal involvement. Tellingly, it occurs through his petition to share the pains of the Mother.

TENTH STANZA

Although implied by the context, suffering is not mentioned in this stanza. It is all about the ardour of love. It is good to note it, lest one think Catholicism has a morbid inclination towards suffering as an end in itself, rather than considering it a powerful means towards our actual goal of union with God.

Verse 28
Fac, ut ardeat cor meum
Make my heart burn

The reader begins to realise that none of his past emotions counted for anything if his heart did not echo the loving beats of the Immaculate Heart of Mary and of the Sacred Heart of Jesus. He now begs Our Lady to obtain for him the spiritual warming of his heart prophesied by Ezekiel long before the Incarnation, and experienced by the Emmaus pilgrims after the Passion and Resurrection of Christ: "*And I will give you a new heart, and put a new spirit within you: and I will take away the stony heart out of your flesh, and will give you a heart of flesh*" (Ezk 36:26) – "*And they said one to the other: Was not our heart burning within us, whilst he spoke in this way, and opened to us the scriptures?"* (*Luke* 24:32).

Verse 29

in amando Christum Deum
with love for Christ, [my] God

This is the middle occurrence of the name 'Christ' out of five in the entire *Stabat Mater*. In verses 14 ('*Matrem Christi*') and 17 ('*Christi Matrem*'), 'Christ' was only mentioned in reference to his Mother. She was the focus of attention, not him. In this verse 29, located in the middle of the sixty-verse poem, Christ is for the first time confessed as God. The word 'God' in fact does not occur anywhere else in the text.

Verse 30

ut sibi complaceam
that I may find grace before Him

The pronoun '*sibi*' ('Him') confirms the gradual shift from the Mother to the Son in the heart of the reader. It is 'his' grace we seek, while 'hers' leads us to 'his'. Because He is God – as just confessed – He is the One whose favour we must win. Far from being left out of our growth in love, his Mother is our safest way to become his.

ELEVENTH STANZA

Verse 31
Sancta Mater, istud agas
O holy mother, this achieve

This is the only occurrence of the adjective 'saint' or 'holy' ('*sancta*') in the *Stabat Mater*. Coming so soon after the confession of Christ as God two verses earlier, it reminds us that the sanctity of the Mother is entirely relative to her Son: her motherly power stems from his divine almightiness. Theologians, therefore, call the Marian devotion 'christocentric' or Christ-centred.

Verse 32
crucifixi fige plagas
impress the wounds of the Crucified One

Pausing for a moment to ponder the objective meaning of this petition, we are shocked by its violence. How can the reader expect the meekest of women to perpetrate such a gory deed? Emphatically, vengeance could not be her motive, even though we sinners would deserve crucifixion inflicted upon us a thousand times for having grievously and pertinaciously offended such a generous and patient Creator. We are spared retribution *only* because the Son of the Mother offered his life in our stead. The Franciscan author of the *Stabat Mater*, Jacopone da Todi would certainly have been inspired here by the miraculous impression of Christ's sacred stigmata upon the four limbs and side of St Francis of Assisi, founder of his mendicant order. We perceive in this verse the slow purification of the reader's emotions. He now wishes to bear the wounds of Christ less out of guilt than out of love.

Verse 33

cordi meo valide
deep in my very heart

Holy Church answers the bitter request of her children as only the best mother would when spreading Holy Chrism upon their limbs and sense organs in the sacrament of Extreme Unction, e.g. on the hands: "*By this holy anointing + and by his most tender mercy may the Lord forgive you all the evil you have done through the sense of touch*". The name 'Christ' means 'the Anointed one'. Thus, the salvific efficacy of the wounds of Christ is applied upon the bodies of dying and sick Christians as if his saving wounds were replicated on their limbs and organs. Furthermore, this duplication of Christ's sacred wounds occurs symbolically as candidates for the Sacred Priesthood receive the clerical Tonsure: the bishop cuts five locks of the seminarian's hair, one for each of

Christ's Five Wounds. Lastly, as the quintuple seal of our redemption, in medieval times the Five Wounds became a sacred emblem carried on banners even to battle for religious freedom as the synthesis of the Christian faith.

TWELFTH STANZA

Verse 34
Tui Nati vulnerati
Of your wounded Begotten One

Instead of the noun 'son' ('*filius*'), which could apply to a man of any age, the participle '*nati*' ('begotten') chosen in this verse expresses more than mere filiation. It movingly hints at the soft and happy lights of the Nativity in Bethlehem – the peaceful intimacy between the Virgin and the Infant and his trusting safety in her arms – in sharp contrast to the dreadful shadows of his present Passion.

Verse 35
tam dignati pro me pati
for He deigned to suffer so much for me

This verse narrows down the identification of the culprit first mentioned in verse 19 from collective to individual. The sinful people – the fallen race of Adam – is replaced by the reader's singular 'me'. The faithful soul becomes overwhelmed by the magnitude of Christ's love for her, which his dire torments manifest.

Verse 36

poenas mecum divide
Let me share with you the pangs

The faithful soul is therefore prompted to ask the Holy Mother to share with her some of her pain, as Christ allowed Simon of Cyrene to carry some of the weight of his Cross. This daring petition indicates a spiritual maturing in the soul. At an earlier stage, she would have shunned involvement in the Mother's suffering, thinking such sharing either irrelevant or presumptuous. Now, trusting not in her strength, but rather in the redemptive power of Christ's sufferings and of her Mother's, the soul thirsts for expiation.

THIRTEENTH STANZA

Verse 37

Fac me tecum pie flere
Grant me to weep lovingly with you

Tears of compassion prove one's heart is alive. The water flows from the eyes of the Holy Mother and of the penitent soul as from one single source.

Verse 38
crucifixo condolere
to feel the pains of the Crucified One

Uniting with the Sorrowful Mother is meant to lead the penitent to sympathise with the divine Son. Again, Catholicism does not see Our Lady as diverting the faithful soul from Christ, but as securely leading one to Him.

Verse 39
donec ego vixero
as long as I live

Because in Latin the personal pronoun is embedded in the verb, nowhere in the *Stabat Mater* do we actually read the word 'I' alone. This verse offers the only occurrence of the nominative personal pronoun '*ego*' in the entire poem, with a strong emphasis on 'I' – 'shall live'. In our thread of the emergence of personal consciousness, the mention of '*ego*' in immediate connection with life duration is encouraging. It confirms that compassion enlivens us. The penitent soul's growing desire to suffer with the Mother and her Son is no lethal trend. On the contrary, it is vivifying.

A richer rhyme connects the three endings of this stanza with those of the previous one: twice '-re, -re, -ro' respectively.

Verse 40

Juxta Crucem tecum stare
To stand with you beside the Cross

By now, plainly and serenely, the penitent soul recognises Calvary as the place of redemption. The tree of the Cross is acknowledged as the new Tree of Life whose branches bear Christ, the Fruit of salvation (and the Author thereof). From her Sorrowful Mother, the New Eve, the contrite soul learns to taste this strange peace found by the Cross: "*As the apple-tree among the trees of the wood, So is my beloved among the sons: In his shadow have I rapture and sit down; And his fruit is sweet to my taste*" (*Songs* 2:3). However, here no one sits. As the Mother stood by the Cross, so does the child now stand by the Mother. The verticality of the Cross was first imitated by the Holy Mother, and now by the penitent soul, as if those became in their turns redemptive trees. Every movement is concentrated in vertical growth, of both roots and branches.

Verse 41

et me tibi sociare
and to be with you united

The soul does not want to leave this place. Calvary becomes her dwelling. No one goes anywhere. For the first time, a verb expresses the bond of affection with the Mother to which the faithful soul aspires: '*sociare*' ('to be united with'). Just as in the primeval garden Eve of old was given by God to Adam as his '*socia*' ('associate'), in the garden of Golgotha the contrite soul seeks admission to the redemptive society of the New Eve with the New Adam. The soul becomes able to stand as spiritual progeny to Jesus and Mary within the new human family.

Verse 42

in planctu desidero
in grief: that, I desire

The soul 'desires' to dwell with Mary and Jesus, as the bride of the Canticle 'desired' to sit down under the shade of the beloved. In passing, let us note the etymology of 'desire' – '*de*' ('from') and '*sideris*' ('of the star'). If 'to desire' is to 'long for a star,' whether for its light or for its warmth, then nowhere better than by the Cross can desires be fulfilled, since the Star of Jacob and true Light of the world shines on that Tree of redemption.

Verse 43

Virgo virginum præclara
Virgin without equal among virgins

While Our Lady is called 'Mother' in eight verses (1, 9, 11, 14, 17, 25, 31, 56), for the first time she is here addressed as 'Virgin', and superlatively, 'virgin of virgins'. This title will occur again only once, in verse 53. This revelation indicates the purification in faith of the penitent soul. She now understands that Mary begets her through redemptive suffering. The penitent soul experiences spiritual adoption. Complementarily, she realises the spiritual motherhood of the Virgin Mother towards her. Confessing Our Lady as 'virgin' implies admission of her divine Motherhood and of her role as co-redemptrix. The penitent soul is led by stages to a deeper appreciation of Our Lady's role in the process of salvation.

Verse 44

mihi iam non sis amara
Be not to me bitter

Strikingly, the name 'Maria' is absent from the *Stabat Mater*. Here it is secretly called for through the mention of the adjective 'Amara' ('bitter') – antithetical to what the Holy Mother is known to be, namely, tender, compassionate and protective. One can implicitly read this petition of the soul to Our Lady ('Be not to me Bitter') as 'Be to me Maria', where 'Bitter' is the antonym of 'Maria' as 'Eva' is to 'Ave' in the inspired pun of the eight century hymn *Ave Maris Stella*. In fact, verse 13 of the *Ave Maris Stella*, "*Show thyself to be a Mother – Monstra te esse Matrem,*" could have inspired this verse 44 of the *Stabat Mater*.

On the other hand, the liturgy of the Church attributes the following words to Our Lady: "*Do not call me Beautiful, but Bitter, for the Almighty has filled me with great bitterness.*" Or in Latin: "*Ne vocétis me pulchram, sed amáram, quia amaritúdine valde replévit me Omnípotens.*" This is the verse after the first lesson of the feast of The Seven Sorrows of the Blessed Virgin Mary (15th September). It is very telling to hear Our Lady choosing for herself the name 'Bitter' in this context. It does not express her attitude towards us, even though we would deserve her bitterness, sinners as we are and cause of her Son's Passion. But the Holy Mother forever remains well disposed towards us. If she asks us to call her 'Bitter' here, or '*Amara*', it is to impress upon us the gravity of our sins. They make her bitter like a spotless mirror reflecting a painful action.

Furthermore, the following episode in the *Book of Exodus* prefigures the role of Our Lady at Calvary. The Hebrew people were dying of thirst after having crossed the Red Sea, until a miracle turned the bitter water of Mara into drinkable water:

> *And Moses brought Israel from the Red Sea, and they went forth into the wilderness of Sur: and they marched three days through the wilderness, and found no water. And they came into Mara, and they could not drink the waters of Mara, because they were bitter: whereupon he gave a name also agreeable to the place, calling it Mara, that is, bitterness. And the people murmured against Moses, saying: "What shall we drink?" But he cried to the Lord, and he shewed him a tree, which when he had cast into the waters, they were turned into sweetness* (*Ex* 15:22-26).

Similarly on Calvary, the multitude of the redeemed received the water of Life from the pierced side of the Crucified, once the tree of the Cross had absorbed the tears of the Most Sorrowful Mother. In *Exodus*, this episode is followed by those of the manna and of the water gushing from the rock struck by Moses. With no claim to etymological accuracy but for the sake of memorising, we could say that 'Mara' becomes 'Mar*I*a' once the shard of the Cross – represented here by the letter 'I' – has pierced the Immaculate Heart.

One could also meditate at length on the Adultery Test in *Numbers* 5:11-31. It decrees that wives suspected of infidelity are asked to drink holy water made bitter through some little earth from the floor of the tabernacle being cast into it with curses. If the woman "*be not defiled, she shall not be hurt, and shall bear children*". No more sacred ground was there ever than the soil in which the Cross was planted, and upon which the Mother stood, mingling her tears with the dust below her. That her Immaculate Heart always belonged to God alone was proven by the fact that she drank the bitter waters of Calvary to the last dregs and yet, begot a multitude of children.

Verse 45

fac me tecum plangere
grant that I may mourn with you

This verse intensifies verse 37 ('Grant me to weep lovingly with you'). What is now asked is not only to share in the Mother's tears but in their cause, i.e., her mourning. After all, tears are only signs of an emotion and as such, they can be shed even by evil people and out of sinful frustration. '*Plangere*' ('mourning') expresses the genuinely virtuous dispositions in the Holy Mother's soul so attuned to her Son's sufferings and his imminent death.

SIXTEENTH STANZA

Verse 46
Fac, ut portem Christi mortem
Grant that I carry about the dying state of Christ

Unlike in previous occurrences, here 'Christ' is not referred to in relation to his Mother anymore, but to his saving death, which the reader wishes to imitate. This anticipates the restoration of the relationship between the penitent soul and Christ the Redeemer completed in Part Three. The victimal condition of Christ as the Lamb of God must be the constant inspiration of our soul, as St Paul teaches: "*Always bearing about in our body the mortification of Jesus, that the life also of Jesus may be made manifest in our bodies*" (*2 Co* 4:10).

Verse 47
passionis fac consortem
grant that I be a sharer in [his] Passion

Inasmuch as we share in Christ's Passion, we are conformed to Him as risen, and we become divinised by grace: "*you may be made partakers of the divine nature: flying the corruption*" (*2 Peter* 1:4).

Verse 48

et plagas recolere
grant that I relive [his] wounds

Our memory must treasure beyond all things the sufferings of Christ for our salvation: "*For I judged not myself to know anything among you, but Jesus Christ, and him crucified*" (*1 Co* 2:2). The regular, indeed daily, meditation on the Passion of the Lord is a most salutary exercise. Since suffering mortifies our nature, the beauty and love of our Sorrowful Mother is a necessary incentive for us to look often towards the Cross, near which she stands. We must pray that the *Stabat Mater* may become the daily guide of Christians praying the Stations of the Cross or merely meditating at home.

SEVENTEENTH STANZA

Verse 49

Fac me plagis vulnerari
Grant that I be wounded with [his] wounds

A secular mind would dismiss this petition as a masochistic desire for self-harm. But at this stage of the *Stabat Mater* we are able to understand it. Christ took upon himself the chastisements we had deserved for our sins: "*Who his own self bore our sins in his Body upon the tree: that we, being dead to sins, should live to justice: by whose stripes you were healed*" (*1 Peter* 2:24). Confessing this truth implies exposing our soul to the spiritual stripes of contrition, in imitation of the Sorrowful (but sinless) Mother.

Verse 50
fac me Cruce inebriari
Let the Cross inebriate me

In the entire hymn, this expression is one of the strongest and most eloquent for its concision. It cannot be understood literally, since inebriation implies consumption of alcohol, whereas the Cross is a solid piece of wood. One cannot drink wood. It calls for a third term, either the Precious Blood of Christ imbibed by the wood, or Christ's Body nailed to the wood, as the 'fruit' pressed to produce the inebriating liquid.

"*But if you partake of the sufferings of Christ, rejoice that when his glory shall be revealed, you may also be glad with exceeding joy*" (*1 Peter* 4:13). The lives of the saints illustrate this paradox of the highest joys found in the deepest humiliations, after the example of the Saviour and of His Mother. This bitter-sweet inebriation was prophesied by Jeremiah: "*He hath filled me with bitterness, he hath inebriated me with wormwood*" (*Lm* 3:15); and by King Solomon: "*Drink, and be inebriated, my dearly beloved*" (*Songs* 5:1).

Verse 51
et cruore Filii
and also the blood of the Son

This verse confirms the inebriating power of the Most Precious Blood of Christ, the price for our redemption: *"it was not with perishable things such as silver or gold that you were redeemed from the empty way of life you inherited from your forefathers, but with the precious blood of Christ"* (*1 Peter* 1:18-19).

EIGHTEENTH STANZA

This last stanza of Part Two steers us towards Part Three, directing our meditation towards judgement and thus, towards Christ as our Judge.

Verse 52
Flammis ne urar successus
That I might not burn and be consumed
in the flames

The choice is between salvation through wilful cleansing of our souls by the blood of Christ or eternal damnation in blazing hell. The choice is not either to burn or not to burn. For burn, we shall. The choice we have is to burn either with charity in heaven or with hatred in hell.

Verse 53
per te, Virgo, sim defensus
Be a defence to me, O Virgin

Against what or whom should Our Lady defend the
soul? Against some implacable enemy? Yes, but more to
be dreaded than its fiercest fiend, *truth* is what the sinful
soul will soon face in the person of Christ, Saviour and
Judge, Who said "*I am the truth*" (*John* 14:6). The role
of Our Lady as Advocate is here ardently stated. Since
"*every man is a liar*" (*Psalm* 116:11), not even saints
can dispense with Our Lady's intercession before Christ
at the end of their lives. However, having crushed the
head of the very Father of Lies, the devil, how could the
Immaculate ever condone any distortion of the truth? If
at judgement our souls are truly found wanting in grace
or merit, how could Our Lady wish to avert retribution?
On the contrary, would not the Seat of Wisdom or '*Sedes
Sapientiæ*' concur with philosophers defining truth, 'The
adequation of the mind with the thing'; where 'the thing'
is our proven guilt, 'the mind' is the divine Logos, and
'the adequation' is judgement passed? Yes, Our Lady will
always stand for and by the truth. She will never wish
our culpability to be declared to be more than it is (as
the devil – the Accuser – would hope), but no less either.

Providentially, though, truth includes her adopting
us at Calvary by her Son's final command. This new

capacity as our adoptive Mother allows her to plead for us before her divine Son. By divine ordinance, Our Lady secures for us acceptance by our Judge. While nothing could be changed to the truth of our insufficiency before Christ, the Virgin Mary is able to mediate between us culprits and the Truth incarnate, that is, between her adopted children and the Son of her flesh. We stand before the Truth as arraigned; but the Mother recommends us to her Son as kindred. Our Lady's motherhood, adoptive as to us and divine as to Christ, achieves this salutary function of making us culprits adequate to the Truth, Jesus our Judge.[6]

As a further illustration, a religious motto states: "*The Mother will take perfect care and be victorious*"; or in Latin, "*Mater perfectam habebit curam et victoriam.*" The "*perfect care*" is her interceding and the "*victory*" is our salvation. It is essential to stress that Our Blessed Lady secures pardon from God on our behalf specifically as our Mother. Accepting, confessing and invoking her motherhood are conditions for sinners to be saved.

---

6 To illustrate this point, we would like to offer here a Latin pun connecting the words 'thing' ('res' in Latin) and 'culprit' ('reus' in Latin), both spelling 'rei' in the Latin genitive. Thus, the definition quoted above, 'The truth is the adequation of the mind with the thing', reads in Latin as follows, 'Adequatio rei et intellectus veritas'. In the moral context of judgement it can be transposed as, 'Adequatio rei et veritatis Maria'; that is, 'Mary is the adequating of the Truth with the culprit'.

God wishes it so because He knows that such a means is best suited to our human nature and to our fallen condition. Ignoring the motherly mediation of Mary as an unnecessary complication, an accident or a mere option, contradicts the merciful Saviour who, as he died on the Cross for our sins, said: "*Woman, behold thy son. After that, he saith to the disciple: Behold thy mother*" (*John* 19:26-27).

Verse 54
in die iudicii
on judgement day

Reckoning will come: "*Be not deceived: God is not mocked. For what things a man shall sow, those also shall he reap. For he that soweth in his flesh of the flesh also shall reap corruption. But he that soweth in the spirit of the spirit shall reap life everlasting*" (*Ga* 6:7-8). Every child of Adam might incur retribution when his life is considered in the light of divine truth: "*I am the Lord who search the heart and prove the reins: who give to every one according to his way, and according to the fruit of his devices*" (*Jr* 17:10). But every sinner must hope for mercy if, admitting his guilt, he trusts in the advocacy of the most Sorrowful Mother who received him as her child at the foot of the Cross. Our Lady will intercede for him, not as if contradicting her Son our Judge, but as fulfilling his providential will to save us through the same Mother He once chose for Himself, so He could become our Brother and make us his kin.

Part Three – Our Mother

This Third and last part of the *Stabat Mater* is surprisingly brief, comprising merely two stanzas against eight (Part One) and ten (Part Two). Far from clumsy, this imbalance is dynamic and artistic. It shows how ninety percent of the poem is meant to prepare the reader for entering this ultimate and most sacred stage. Keeping the Mother in mind, we could compare the *Stabat Mater* with the iceberg, whose visible tip above water amounts to only ten percent of its total volume. The first eighteen stanzas (ninety percent of the poem) are about Our Lady and only the last two about Our Lord. He is the focus and the destination. She remains hidden as a humble means, as if under water. But just as shipwreck explorers only find refuge on the visible tip of the floating iceberg thanks to its much larger part immersed, penitents only rest in Christ thanks to the discreet mediation of his and their Mother. The shift from Part Two to Part Three completes the moral resurrection of the soul, finally getting out of the deadly waters of self-justification after swimming upward towards the surface.

The composition of the *Stabat Mater* could also be compared to the structure of the Tabernacle of Moses in the desert during the Exodus, whose threefold plan was retained (albeit extended) later in the Temple in Jerusalem. In either case, the ultimate and smallest of the three parts, the Holy of Holies, could only be accessed through two larger spaces, the Outer Courtyard and the Holy Place. Like our Jewish forefathers in the Old Testament, we, the Easter People, have access secured to Christ, our Holy of Holies, through the mediation of the Sorrowful Mother.

NINETEENTH STANZA

Verse 55
Christe, cum sit hinc exire
O Christ, when I must depart hence

Climactically, Christ is addressed directly (*'Christe'*) for the first time, using the vocative case expressive of a personal relationship, unlike the genitive and the accusative used in previous mentions of 'Christ'.

The Sorrowful Mother has successfully accomplished her mission if :

1) the penitent soul now understands that Christ owns her, having redeemed her from the tyranny of Satan at the cost of his Precious Blood;

2) the soul loves her Redeemer enough to dare address Him directly. This is happening in this verse. Let us not take this step for granted. It has taken 54 verses to lead us gently to that depth of contrition and that height of confidence. It has taken the pitiful display of the sufferings of the most beautiful and innocent of mothers, in association with those of her divine Son.

Verse 56
da per Matrem me venire
give me through the mother to seize

The soul has not forgotten the mediation of her Holy Mother. It is again through and of Mary that the humble penitent expects to receive salvation from her Son. This verse is a summary of Catholicism in its entirety. The imperative form '*da*' ('grant') connects confidently the child and Christ, but through the mediation of the Mother. Some translators insert a possessive article before 'Mother', i.e.: 'through *your* mother'. This is accurate inasmuch as Christ is the Son of Mary. But it is too restrictive since the whole hymn aims at making us realise that Mary is also our Mother. A better interpretation therefore would be: 'through *our* mother', that is, Christ's and mine, as himself spoke of his Father: "*Go to my brethren, and say to them: I ascend to my Father and to your Father, to my God and your God*" (*John* 20:17).

Verse 57
ad palmam victoriæ
the palm of victory

The abysmal humiliations of the divine Messiah in his Passion led to his blessed Resurrection and his glorious Ascension. His members will follow their Head through these stages. Victory is the end. But as depicted in images of martyrdom, the palm of triumph is often dipped in blood. Although most Christians do not die martyrs, all have their "*old man crucified with* [Christ]" (*Rm* 6:6).

TWENTIETH STANZA

Out of twenty stanzas in the *Stabat Mater*, this last one is the only one whose final verse fails to rhyme with the last verse of the previous stanza: '-ia' instead of '-iæ'. This minor lack of symmetry singling out the very last verse of the entire poem conveys a sense of incompletion, poetically speaking. It could be intended to foster a longing for the fulfilment of redemption only secured through the reader's saintly death.

Verse 58
Quando corpus morietur
When my body is dead

Having for so long contemplated the dying Lord, having seen his sacred Body taken down from the Cross and put in the lap of his Mother, penitents can face the prospect of their own dead body. Yes, our soul will depart from it and our flesh will decay before both are united again at the Last Judgement.

Verse 59

fac, ut animæ donetur
grant that my soul be given

This is the last occurrence out of nine of the imperative *'fac'* ('grant'). The first eight were addressed to the Blessed Mother; this last one to her Son. It gathers the impetuous confidence accumulated in the first eight petitions to the Holy Mother. Surely, without this Marian preparation, the sinner would not have dared to address the divine Son with such boldness.

Verse 60

paradisi gloria. Amen
the glory of paradise. Amen

Eventually, the soul confesses that the holy will of God is nothing other than her salvation: "*For this is the will of God, your sanctification*" (*1 Th* 4:3). The ignominies of Calvary obtained for the soul heavenly glories, to be forever enjoyed in the bosom of the Most Holy Trinity. Now rejoicing, the Mother introduces the soul to the Triune God, as invited by the Five Wounds forever shining in the sacred humanity she gave to the Son.

Conclusion

The *Stabat Mater* purges our fallen ego fatally inflated by pride. Our swollen ego is shrunk to nothingness in Part One while witnessing the sufferings of the Woman. It awakens through Marian filiation in Part Two. It is fully restored to life in Part Three, through kinship with the divine Son of Mary, our Redeemer. This healing process is cathartic. It prompts emotions in us, turning them from sentimental and selfish to compassionate and altruistic. Admittedly, we should not base our spiritual life on emotions, for those come and go. Emotions are not always under our control. They can be deceptive. On the other hand, feelings are part and parcel of our human nature. Our Lord himself wept on several occasions, displayed anger, and experienced friendship and sympathy. From Our Lord and Our Lady, then, we must learn the ordered use of emotions. Chiefly in the *Stabat Mater*, we learn to grieve with Our Lady for the pains of her Son, Our Lord. Our grief then is not superficial or narcissistic. It is a fitting, necessary and salutary expression of our guilt as sinners. Our Lord once stated that we have hearts of stone. Pride makes it difficult for us to feel for others. The *Stabat Mater* trains us in sympathising at the deepest level. This is the condition for salvation. Unless we freely recognise that Christ suffered for the sins we committed, his Passion and Cross cannot save us from hell. But if we look at the most beautiful of Mothers weeping for the most innocent of Sons, we are likely to learn true sympathy, contrition and hope: "O most Sorrowful Mother, make our hearts alike to thine. From your Son, obtain for us life everlasting."

To 'stand with' the Mother at the Cross of the Son is the only effective protection against the formal rejection of the faith or apostasy, a noun which literally means 'to stand apart'. 'Standing with' the Sorrowful Mother is also the surest guarantee of rising again to heavenly glory, which the Greek calls 'anastasis' (hence the female name 'Anastasia', i.e. 'Resurrection'). 'Standing with' the Mother to encounter her Son secures our transit from sin to grace and furthers our passage from grace to glory. Pivotal is its position between sin and glory, supporting our passage from apostasy to 'anastasy'. Let us see how. The first 'apo-stasy' or 'standing-apart' was the Original Sin. Its immediate symptom was Adam and Eve's withdrawing from God's presence on hearing Him come in the Garden of Eden, as they *"hid themselves from the face of the Lord God"* (*Gn* 3:8). On Easter morning, the blessed Resurrection of Jesus or 'ana-stasy' is what God wants for all children of Adam and Eve: that we stand redeemed by the New Adam, Our Lord, assisted by the New Eve, Our Lady. But how can we sinners transition from apostasy to anastasy, that is, from fallen to risen? How to bridge the gap of sin and leap into grace? There has to be a missing link or segment between apostasy and anastasy. What is it? As we know, Christ the Redeemer is the One who merited for us everlasting life through his Passion and death on the Cross. But He gave us his Immaculate Mother to help us apply his merits to our needs. How does she achieve this? Through her 'standing-by' the Cross. As the title and first verse of the hymn stress, Our Lady stood by the Cross in sorrow. This is our missing link between apostasy and anastasy, between fall and resurrection. Fittingly, we could define it as 'matri-stasy', literally, the 'Mother's-standing-by [the-Cross]'. The *Stabat Mater* develops this vital intermediary stage,[7] namely the compassionate and fecund standing-by of the Mother, that is, the intermediary stage in our journey from fall to rise.

---

[7] Taking the word 'stasy' ('station', from 'to stand') as our substantive, we may conveniently shift before it the three prefixes 'apo-' ('off'), 'matri-', ('[Mother]-by') and 'ana-' ('up'). At school, students learn ways to simplify complex arithmetical equations. As a theological equivalent to help us memorise the dynamic of the *Stabat Mater*, we offer the following equation: *off* ÷ *by* = *up*. It is based on the explanation given above, articulating the three stages of human history around the substantive 'stasy' ('to stand').

Finally, we may consider the *Stabat Mater* to have a fourth part. Not that one should presume to improve this most celebrated Catholic hymn, a literary crucible whereby children of wrath are shaped into heirs to the Kingdom, and sons of perdition into channels of grace. Rather, the proposed Part Four is already written as Part One. Our patient and thorough meditation of the full poem now rewards us with a new understanding of its beginning.

A second reading of stanzas one to four (that is, before the first mention of Christ in stanza five) shows us that every sinner is the son or daughter over whom the Sorrowful Mother weeps. She knows that her Son Jesus would have endured all these torments even to save one soul only. She also knows that none of these tortures would have occurred unless salvation was at stake. When, standing by the Cross, Our Lady looked at her Son, it was therefore ultimately *us* sinners whom she sought and for whom she prayed. Such was the will of her Son. On the Cross, she sees *us* hanging, bleeding, and groaning.

The *Stabat Mater* is understood and well prayed only when allowing the Holy Mother to look at our souls as once disfigured by sin and causing the pains of her Son and herself – or as redeemed from sin, through the pains of her Son and herself. Then we truly become her children, she our Mother, and He our Brother Redeemer.

"O Sorrowful Mother, plead for us thy children, whom thou didst receive and accept at the foot of the Cross!"

Through her intercession, we hope to be admitted among the countless saints who, in spirit, joined Our Lady, St John and St Mary Magdalene at Calvary, as portrayed by the Collect on the Commemoration of the Seven Sorrows of the Blessed Virgin Mary: *"by the glorious merits and prayers of all the Saints who faithfully stood beneath the Cross interceding for us,"* – that we might rise again to eternal life in Christ her Son Our Lord.

Text of the *Stabat Mater*

Unlike our rendition above adapted from various translations, the following translation by Fr Edward Caswall CO (1814-1878) is not literal. We include it below for the reader's devotion. It represents the trochaic tetrameter rhyme scheme, and sense of the original text.

STABAT Mater dolorosa,
Juxta Crucem lacrimosa,
dum pendebat Filius.

AT, the Cross her station keeping,
stood the mournful Mother weeping,
close to Jesus to the last.

Cuius animam gementem,
contristatam et dolentem,
pertransivit gladius.

Through her heart, His sorrow sharing,
all His bitter anguish bearing,
now at length the sword has passed.

O quam tristis et afflicta
fuit illa benedicta,
mater Unigeniti!

O how sad and sore distressed
was that Mother, highly blest,
of the sole-begotten One!

Quae maerebat et dolebat,
pia Mater, dum videbat
nati poenas inclyti.

Christ above in torment hangs,
she beneath beholds the pangs
of her dying glorious Son.

Quis est homo qui non fleret,
Matrem Christi si videret,
in tanto supplicio?

Is there one who would not weep,
whelmed in miseries so deep,
Christ's dear Mother to behold?

Quis non posset contristari
Christi Matrem contemplari,
dolentem cum Filio?

Can the human heart refrain
from partaking in her pain,
in that Mother's pain untold?

Pro peccatis suae gentis,
vidit Iesum in tormentis,
et flagellis subditum.

Bruised, derided, cursed, defiled,
she beheld her tender Child,
all with bloody scourges rent.

Vidit suum dulcem Natum,
moriendo desolatum,
dum emisit spiritum.

For the sins of His own nation,
saw Him hang in desolation,
till His spirit forth He sent.

Eia, Mater! Fons amoris!
me sentire vim doloris,
fac, ut tecum lugeam.

O thou Mother! Fount of love!
Touch my spirit from above,
make my heart with thine accord:

Fac, ut ardeat cor meum;
in amando Christum Deum
ut sibi complaceam.

Make me feel as thou hast felt;
make my soul to glow and melt
with the love of Christ my Lord.

Sancta Mater! Istud agas,
crucifixi fige plagas
cordi meo valide.

Holy Mother! Pierce me through,
in my heart each wound renew
of my Saviour crucified.

Tui Nati vulnerati,
tam dignati pro me pati,
poenas mecum divide.

Let me share with thee His pain,
who for all my sins was slain,
who for me in torments died.

Fac me tecum pie flere,
crucifixo condolere,
donec ego vixero.

Let me mingle tears with thee,
mourning Him who mourned for me,
all the days that I may live.

Juxta Crucem tecum stare,	By the Cross with thee to stay,
et me tibi sociare,	there with thee to weep and pray,
in planctu desidero.	is all I ask of thee to give.
Virgo virginum praeclara!	Virgin of all virgins blest!,
Mihi iam non sis amara:	Listen to my fond request:
fac me tecum plangere.	let me share thy grief divine.
Fac, ut portem Christi mortem,	Let me, to my latest breath,
passionis fac consortem	in my body bear the death
et plagas recolere.	of that dying Son of thine.
Fac me plagis vulnerari,	Wounded with His every wound,
fac me Cruce inebriari,	steep my soul till it hath swooned,
et cruore Filii.	in His very Blood away.
Flammis ne urar succensus,	Be to me, O Virgin, nigh,
per te, Virgo, sim defensus,	lest in flames I burn and die,
in die iudicii.	in His awful Judgement Day.
Christe, cum sit hinc exire,	Christ, when Thou shalt call me hence,
da per Matrem me venire,	by Thy Mother my defense,
ad palmam victoriae.	by Thy Cross my victory;
Quando corpus morietur,	While my body here decays,
fac, ut animae donetur,	may my soul Thy goodness praise,
paradisi gloria. Amen.	safe in paradise with Thee. Amen.